SENECA PUBLIC LIBRARY DISTRICT

W9-AZG-322

SENECA LIBRARY DISTRICT

SEP 2 7 2010

SOUTH CAROLINA

Past and Present

Daniel E. Harmon

rosen publishing's
rosen
central®

New York

Published in 2011 by The Rosen Publishing Group, Inc.
29 East 21st Street, New York, NY 10010

Copyright © 2011 by The Rosen Publishing Group, Inc.

First Edition

All rights reserved. No part of this book may be reproduced in any form without permission in writing from the publisher, except by a reviewer.

Library of Congress Cataloging-in-Publication Data

Harmon, Daniel E.
South Carolina: past and present / Daniel E. Harmon. — 1st ed.
    p. cm. — (The United States: past and present)
Includes bibliographical references and index.
ISBN 978-1-4358-9495-2 (library binding)
ISBN 978-1-4358-9522-5 (pbk.)
ISBN 978-1-4358-9556-0 (6-pack)
1. South Carolina—Juvenile literature. I. Title.
F269.3.H36 2010
975.7—dc22

                                                                    2010002586

Manufactured in Malaysia

CPSIA Compliance Information: Batch #S10YA: For further information, contact Rosen Publishing, New York, New York, at 1-800-237-9932.

On the cover: Top left: Children work in a South Carolina cotton mill in 1903. Top right: The newly reinforced Lake Murray Dam (also known as Saluda Dam) is used for generating hydroelectricity. Bottom: The Congaree National Park enables visitors to encounter a variety of wildlife, including river otters and wild pigs, and tall trees, such as bald cypresses and water tupelos, in its floodplain ecosystem.

Contents

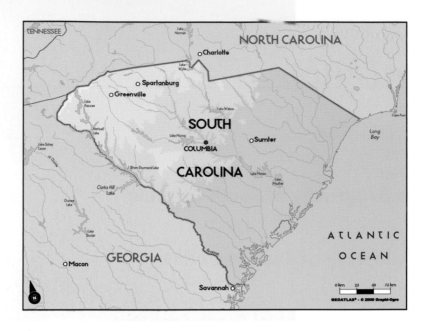

South Carolina is roughly three-sided, in the shape of an upside-down pyramid. Its southwestern border is the Atlantic Ocean. Georgia is its southwestern neighbor, and North Carolina is its northern. Columbia is its capital. One of the nation's smallest states, it ranks fortieth in size.

Introduction

"While I breathe, I hope." That is South Carolina's historic motto, translated from Latin. The modern slogan adopted by the state's department of parks, recreation, and tourism is "Smiling Faces. Beautiful Places." Both phrases describe South Carolina. It was a land of hope for the first European explorers and settlers. It still is for their descendants, for the Native American societies that remain, and for new residents who arrive from around the world.

South Carolina is a small state that has had a big effect on American history. Located on the Atlantic Seaboard, the area was an entry point for European immigrants during colonial times. The colony played a vital role in the American Revolution. Later, the state led the secession movement that exploded into the Civil War.

In modern times, South Carolina has produced a special tapestry of Americans: sun-browned farmers, business and industry leaders, astronauts, civil rights activists, educators, entertainers, and presidential advisers. Most South Carolinians through the centuries have been much like the citizens of other states. They are hardworking, friendly Americans. They are little known outside the towns where they live and their small circles of distant friends and relatives. Regardless, they contribute greatly to the nation's well-being and progress.

THE GEOGRAPHY OF SOUTH CAROLINA

Chapter 1

Tourism officials and historians use an interesting phrase to describe South Carolina: "From the mountains to the sea." It refers to the state's remarkable range of geographical features.

South Carolina's terrain is divided into three regions, which can be divided further into six geographical bands. These zones stretch between the Georgia border on the southwest and the North Carolina border in the north and northeast.

The Coastal Plain—the lower half of the state—consists of three of the bands. The Coastal Zone extends along the Atlantic Coast for about 20 miles (32 kilometers) inland. It is especially notable for the many sea (barrier) islands. Sea islands serve as helpful natural protection from the ocean's occasional wrath. This zone is bordered by the Outer Coastal Plain. Next is the Inner Coastal Plain, which reaches to the midlands.

The Sandhills, a thin line of sand-covered land across the center of the state, begins the broad Piedmont region. The Piedmont covers the upstate to within sight of the Blue Ridge Mountains.

The mountains themselves are in the Blue Ridge geographical zone. This is a small section in the northwestern corner of South Carolina.

The Coastal Plain and Sandhills tell an interesting story. Geologists say the ocean, millions of years ago, covered the lower half of what

6

Table Rock, in the Blue Ridge Mountains, is a well-known landmark in northwestern South Carolina. Adventurous climbers have attempted (illegally) to scale the looming rock face—sometimes with fatal results.

is now South Carolina. The sandy land that forms the Sandhills was once beachfront and dunes.

A Fertile, Bountiful State

From the coast to the mountains, South Carolina has rich soil. It produces magnificent crops, and it's healthy. In 1930, a radio station in Columbia took "WIS" as its call letters. They stood for "wonderful iodine state." South Carolina's dirt is rich in iodine. This chemical reduces the likelihood of goiters. A goiter is a horrible throat growth that was common before modern medicine was developed.

The Ocean and Land

Europeans who tried to colonize the area in the 1500s were thwarted by distrustful Native Americans and unhealthy conditions. Malaria and other diseases bred in the marshy, swampy Low Country. Summertime toil was extremely hot and sweaty. The sea brought the newcomers here, but they found seaside living quite tough.

Today, coastal retirees and visitors don't worry about malaria. They don't have to sweat in diseased, swampy fields. They love the ocean. They sunbathe, play golf and tennis at nearby resorts, shop in convenient malls, and thoroughly enjoy seaside living.

But today's coastal residents face difficulties, too. They can't protect themselves from the hurricanes that have pounded the region throughout history. Their problems are even more complicated. Property buyers have invested heavily here. Beachfront property, highly valued not long ago, has become a risky investment. Nature is eroding some of the once-broad beaches. South Carolina fishers, whose families have relied on the Atlantic for many generations, are hindered by dwindling catches.

Atlantic surf is churned up by storm-force winds. South Carolina's beautiful beaches can be perilous in hurricane season.

The warm climate and fertile land attracted Europeans here almost five hundred years ago. Early settlers labored to clear forests for small farms and large plantations.

Despite population growth and other changes, most of the state remains woodlands. Private landowners have most of the forests. Other woodlands are state or federal reserves. South Carolina is known for its pine woods, sprawling oaks, magnolias, and many other tree varieties. The state tree, the palmetto, is found in coastal areas. Dozens of wildflowers are common in South Carolina. They include yellow jessamine, rhododendron, mountain laurel, and dogwood.

South Carolina is home to four poisonous snake species. This timber rattler's home is in the Congaree National Park, 15 miles (24 km) from the state capital.

Animals frequently seen in the wild include white-tailed deer, squirrels, rabbits, chipmunks, beavers, red foxes, bears, coyotes, turkeys, and hundreds of birds, insects, reptiles, and amphibians. Birds (more than a hundred species) range from large predators like the bald eagle, hawk, and owl to small species such as the wren and sparrow. Wild waterfowl—pelicans, ducks, Canada geese, cranes, ospreys, and others—fascinate birders.

Many snake species thrive in South Carolina. Poisonous snakes are rattlesnakes, cottonmouth moccasins, copperheads, and corals. Alligators abound, especially in watery environments in the lower half of the state. Fishers eagerly pursue both freshwater (bass, catfish, trout, and various pan fish) and saltwater (barracuda, tuna, sea bass, and many other) species.

Ancient Rivers, Modern Lakes, Geographical Oddities

South Carolina is divided by several river systems. Most rivers flow from northwest to southeast, emptying into the Atlantic Ocean. The Savannah River forms the 240-mile (386 km) border between South Carolina and Georgia.

The Broad River, flowing down from North Carolina, is enlarged by several smaller upstate rivers. In the midlands, they become the Congaree, which merges with the Wateree as it enters the coastal area, called the Low Country. This union forms the Santee River system—the most extensive river system along the Atlantic Coast.

South Carolina's major lakes are man-made. Their purpose is to generate electrical power. In 1919, a power company dammed the Wateree River to form Lake Wateree. Other projects followed over the next sixty years. When completed in 1930 on the Saluda River, about 10 miles (16 km) above Columbia, the Lake Murray dam was the longest earthen dam in the world.

Unusual natural features are seen in different parts of the state. Peachtree Rock in rural Lexington County is a huge, delicately perched sandstone formation in the shape of an upside-down pyramid—much like the shape of the state. A small waterfall (extraordinary, in the Sandhills zone) is nearby.

Forty-Acre Rock in Lancaster County is likewise curious. Basically, it is a big slab of granite. A remarkable variety of plants, including rare and endangered species, take root there.

Poinsett State Park is another curiosity. Although it is located in the relatively flat Coastal Plain, its hills and vegetation resemble the mountains. It was named after South Carolinian Joel R. Poinsett (1779–1851), a U.S. statesman and naturalist.

The Congaree National Park in Richland County contains a rare forest of hardwood trees. Some species are the largest still existing in the United States.

Pleasures and Dangers

The state's climate is subtropical. It generally is mild—not nearly as cold during the winter as in northern states or as hot during the summer as in the Southwest. For that reason, it has lured seasonal residents for two centuries. During the late 1800s, wealthy northerners adopted Aiken as a "winter colony." They indulged in horse racing, polo, tennis, and golf while their friends back home braced against ice. Aiken is still famous as a training ground for world-class racehorses.

The state's natural springs have been another drawing card. Many spring locations became resorts. Some, like Glenn Springs in Spartanburg County, attracted rich summer visitors by rail from across South Carolina and faraway states until the 1920s. They believed Glenn Springs water cured various illnesses. (Actually, it was high in sulfur content. It tasted awful and had little healing effect—except to flush their digestive systems and send them running to the toilet.)

Year-round residents witness unpleasant features of the state's location, too. South Carolina has weathered its share of Atlantic hurricanes. The severest in recent history was Hurricane Hugo, a massive storm that centered its fury on Charleston in 1989. Winds exceeded 150 miles (241 km) per hour. Hugo was just one of many vicious tempests. In 1752, a strong hurricane struck Charles Town in mid-September. Another followed in its path two weeks later. With almost no warning, the "Great Storm of 1893" slammed into the Sea Islands, killing more than two thousand people. Almost every year, a hurricane damages South Carolina.

Hurricane Hugo in September 1989 was one of the most destructive in U.S. history. Many South Carolina coastal residents mark the events of time generally as "before Hugo" and "after Hugo."

South Carolina does not have as many earthquakes as its West Coast counterpart, California. Like California, though, it is dangerously "faulted." It lies atop a geologic fault beneath Earth's surface. This means it can experience catastrophic earthquakes. In 1886, a quake damaged most of the structures in Charleston, totally destroying many of them. Sixty people died. It's estimated that more than fourteen thousand chimneys were toppled. The damage was $23 million, which would be calculated in billions today. The U.S. Geological Survey rates it as the worst recorded earthquake in the Southeast and "one of the great earthquakes in United States history."

Chapter 2

THE HISTORY OF SOUTH CAROLINA

In the summer of 1521, a Spanish ship commanded by Francisco Gordillo anchored off what is now the South Carolina coast. These Spaniards did not come to the New World to settle, search for gold, or look for a short sea route between the Atlantic and Pacific oceans. Their mission was cruel. Spain needed slaves to work its plantations and mines on Caribbean islands. Gordillo tricked Chicora Indians aboard his vessel, offering them gifts—and then bound them and sailed away.

For thousands of years, the Chicora and other peoples had occupied the area. Indian women farmed, growing corn, beans, and squash. The men hunted and trapped wild game and fished for food. The largest native groups were the Cherokee and Catawba.

About thirty Indian groups inhabited the area when the Europeans arrived. Some of the ancient societies were Mound Builders. They built earthworks for ceremonial purposes. Some were not much larger than a grave site. Others were huge, more than 50 feet (15.25 meters) high. Archaeologists have identified dozens of mound sites in South Carolina. Most have almost disappeared because of erosion, but others are still visible. Many of the mounds, such as Minin Island Shell Midden in Georgetown County and Santee Indian Mound in Clarendon County, are protected by the state or federal government.

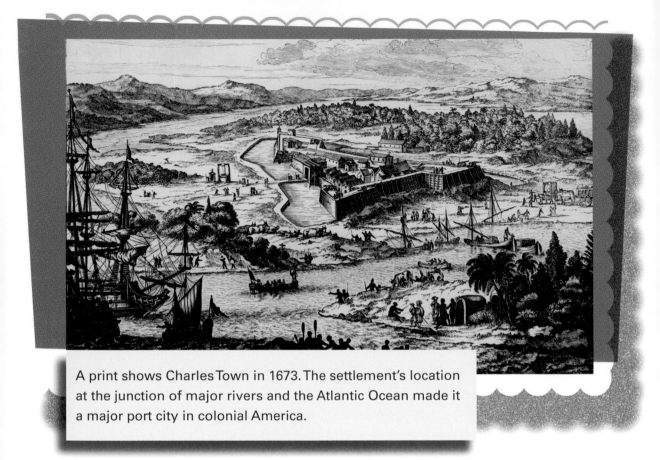

A print shows Charles Town in 1673. The settlement's location at the junction of major rivers and the Atlantic Ocean made it a major port city in colonial America.

European Settlements

Five years after Gordillo's raid, other Spanish expeditions began arriving. They were looking for gold and trading goods. The early Spaniards established crude forts and settlements, but they did not survive. Malaria and other marsh diseases, attacks by unfriendly Indians, and other hardships drove the newcomers away. French settlements also failed. Not until 1670 did the Europeans succeed with a permanent settlement. An English group forged it at Port Royal, near the small modern-day port of Beaufort.

The English named the territory Carolana (later Carolina) after their king, Charles I. It covered a vast area that included what is today North and South Carolina. The territory was divided in 1712, and the two Carolinas became separate English colonies in 1729.

By then, many settlements had been established. The most prosperous was Charles Town (now Charleston). It was an ideal seaport, positioned in a protected harbor where two rivers flowed into the Atlantic. Trading goods were floated downriver from inland posts and shipped to Europe. At the same time, vessels from across the Atlantic brought an increasing number of immigrants and supplies to the new colony.

Poor farm families came because they wanted to work their own land and escape religious persecution in Europe. Tanners, blacksmiths, and other tradesmen knew they could find work in the growing settlements. Merchants were eager to make their fortunes. The newcomers were willing to endure many hardships: heavy labor, deadly diseases, raids by Native Americans, and frequent river flooding. Charles Town was half destroyed by a fire in 1698. Pirates often attacked ports and ships.

Dependence on Slavery

Not all settlers were poor. Wealthy Englishmen established sprawling plantations throughout the fertile Low Country. They took advantage of the region's warm, humid climate and tidal flooding to cultivate rice. Soon, rice was the colony's most valuable export to Europe. Planters also began to produce large crops of indigo and, later, cotton.

To grow large quantities of these crops, planters needed cheap labor. Their solution was slavery. At first, they sent slaving parties

South Carolina's Military Prominence

The palmetto, South Carolina's state tree, gives the state its nickname. South Carolina military history buffs are especially proud of it. During the Revolutionary War, a British fleet tried to capture Charles Town. The two forts that guarded Charles Town Harbor were walled with soft palmetto logs and mud. The spongy wood absorbed the warships' cannon balls, and the British attack failed.

Seventy-five years later, Charleston Harbor was the scene of the first military action of the Civil War. Confederates bombarded Fort Sumter. Charleston became a key Confederate supply port, but the U.S. Navy blockaded the harbor. The Confederate Navy responded by using blockade-runners, fast sailing vessels that could dodge the blockade. It also experimented with new weapons. The *H. L. Hunley*, a small, hand-powered submarine, was the first in history to sink an enemy warship. It destroyed a blockading vessel and, in the process, sank itself. Divers found the *Hunley* wreck in 1995; it was brought to the surface in 2000.

Many South Carolinians have served as national military leaders. They span the years from Andrew Pickens and Francis Marion during the Revolution, William Barrett Travis at the Alamo, and Secretary of War Joel R. Poinsett in the 1830s to Vietnam commander William Westmoreland in the 1960s.

Today, the state plays a crucial part in maintaining the nation's military power. Besides numerous military bases located here (including Charleston Air Force Base, Fort Jackson, and South Carolina National Guard), an academy in Charleston, The Citadel, has trained future army officers since 1842.

into the interior to bring back Indian captives. By 1700, most slaves were being captured in Africa and shipped to America in chains, packed tightly in the holds of rickety, filthy transatlantic vessels. It has been estimated that as many as twenty in one hundred died during the long voyages. Those who arrived alive were sold to plantation owners.

South Carolina at War

South Carolinians, beginning in 1765, joined other colonists in opposing a series of taxes that the English Parliament imposed on them. The English government tried to tax the purchase of newspapers, tea, glass, and even playing cards. It also charged taxes for importing and exporting such goods as furs, indigo, coffee, and sugar. Angry colonists refused to buy English goods. Tensions increased. Colonial representatives, including leading statesmen from South Carolina—Thomas Heyward Jr., Thomas Lynch Jr., Arthur Middleton, and Edward Rutledge—declared independence from England in 1776. This began the American Revolution.

Not all South Carolinians wanted independence. Some, called Loyalists or Tories, believed they were better off under English rule. More Revolutionary War battles and skirmishes were fought in South Carolina than in any other colony. Many of them did not involve regular soldiers but pitted Tories against Patriots. In some cases, neighbors and even close relatives fought against one another. That's why the Revolution has been called America's first civil war.

By 1780, the British seemed to be winning the war. However, the Americans won important battles in South Carolina at Kings Mountain in October 1780 and Cowpens the following January. Great Britain's

The U.S. Army controlled Fort Sumter in Charleston Harbor in 1861. When the Southern states seceded, Southern forces bombarded and captured the offshore fort, starting the Civil War.

southern army withdrew northward. British troops were forced to surrender at Yorktown, Virginia, which effectively ended the American Revolution.

South Carolina became the first state to secede from the Union in December 1860. Four months later, Confederate gunners forced Union soldiers to surrender Fort Sumter in Charleston.

A Long, Painful Recovery

The South was in shambles after the war. Many cities, towns, and farms had been burned by conquering Northern forces. Both whites and blacks toiled to survive. Under the Reconstruction government, which was enforced by the U.S. Army, blacks enjoyed newfound freedoms. For a while, they held political power. Some Southern whites bitterly opposed Reconstruction policies. The Ku Klux Klan, organized by former Confederate soldiers, intimidated blacks, often violently.

Reconstruction ended with the election of Wade Hampton, a former Confederate general, as South Carolina's governor in 1876. Hampton and most other whites opposed the Republican Party that had been led by Abraham Lincoln. Hampton's election began a century of political control of South Carolina by the Democrats.

Democrats were not united. Many struggling farmers considered Hampton, a member of the wealthy class, unsympathetic to their concerns. In 1890, a populist Democrat named Benjamin "Pitchfork Ben" Tillman was elected governor. Tillman opposed powerful commercial interests. He also resisted black citizens' efforts toward equality. A confusing tension among races, social classes, and economic interest groups drove state politics until the late twentieth century.

The Twentieth Century

The cotton mill era brought much-needed progress to the state from

Jesse Jackson of Greenville was a key activist in the civil rights movement. His national standing took him on the presidential campaign trail in the 1980s.

the late 1800s until the late 1900s. However, many rural South Carolinians lived in poverty. Soil erosion and crop blights drove thousands of poor farm families, most of them blacks, from the state.

The state changed dramatically in politics and social views during the late twentieth century. Segregation—the public separation of white and black people—existed nationwide before the Civil War. Segregation policies lingered in some northern areas until the 1900s but were most obvious in the South. Southern blacks boldly challenged separation policies after World War II (1939–1945). Their efforts became known as the civil rights movement. South Carolinians were among the civil rights leaders of the 1950s and 1960s. They included Jesse Jackson, a Greenville native who became a presidential candidate.

During this time, key political leaders and millions of South Carolina voters switched from the Democratic Party to the Republican Party. James B. Edwards in 1974 was the first Republican elected South Carolina governor since the 1800s.

The last half of the twentieth century was a boom time for the economy. New industries provided thousands of jobs in a state that had relied mainly on agriculture for three hundred years. They brought new citizens, relocating from other states and countries. With them came a variety of cultural contributions.

South Carolina today is a past-and-present state. Its people preserve its history and take pride in its progress.

Chapter 3

THE GOVERNMENT OF SOUTH CAROLINA

South Carolina is divided into forty-six counties. It has almost three hundred cities and towns.

At local levels, each county and municipality has a government system that handles matters directly affecting people's lives. County citizens elect councils, sheriffs, treasurers, court clerks, and other officers. County taxes pay for law enforcement, fire and rescue services, education, work done on county roads, building inspections, and many other services. Cities and most towns elect mayors and councils. Municipal taxes pay for government services inside city/town limits such as police and fire protection, garbage collection, local building inspections, and zoning enforcement.

Three Branches of Government

State government consists of three branches: executive, legislative, and judicial. Although the state was founded in the 1700s, the constitution that was adopted in 1895 is its basis of government. Most government offices are located in and near the state house in Columbia.

At the head of the executive branch is the governor. Governors are elected to four-year terms and may serve two consecutive terms.

The domed state house in Columbia is the state's third capitol building, completed in 1903. It was greatly restored in the late 1990s.

The governor appoints fifteen executive cabinet members who serve as the heads of state agencies (department of commerce, department of motor vehicles, department of social services, state law enforcement division, etc.).

Other statewide executive officials are elected to four-year terms. Known as constitutional officers, they include the lieutenant governor, secretary of state, treasurer, attorney general, comptroller general, superintendent of education, commissioner of agriculture, and adjutant general.

The legislative branch is the general assembly. It consists of the South Carolina House of Representatives (124 members) and Senate (46 members). Representatives are elected to two-year terms, senators to four-year terms. The main function of the legislature is to make and revise laws.

At the top of the judicial branch is the South Carolina Supreme Court. Supreme court justices are elected by the legislature to ten-year terms. The court consists of four associate justices and a chief justice. They make the rules that apply to South Carolina's lower courts. They hear appeals in cases that end in circuit court death sentences. Also, they decide who can become a lawyer in South Carolina.

African Americans in South Carolina Government

Until the Civil War ended slavery, African Americans could not vote and took no part in South Carolina government. In 1867, the federal Reconstruction Acts gave all adults the right to vote. African Americans then made up 60 percent of the voting population. They supported the Republican Party, which backed improved conditions for freedmen. Numerous blacks were elected to the state general assembly and the U.S. Congress.

The new state government became marred by corruption. White-backed Democratic candidates regained control in the election of 1876. For the next century, African Americans had little political power in South Carolina.

The success of the civil rights movement during the 1950s and 1960s led to renewed African American strength in state politics. Herbert U. Fielding and I. S. Leevy Johnson were elected to the South Carolina House of Representatives in 1970, becoming the first African Americans to take legislative seats since 1895. Four years later, Juanita W. Goggins became the first black woman ever elected to the house. In 1983, the Reverend I. DeQuincy Newman became the first African American state senator since the late 1800s. Maggie Glover in 1992 became the first black woman elected to the state senate. The same year, James Clyburn became the state's first African American U.S. congressman in modern times.

Today, African American influence in state government continues to expand. Although they have not yet won a constitutional office, black candidates frequently run for executive positions, including governor.

Locally, circuit courts, municipal courts, family courts, probate courts, and magistrate courts hear and try cases. A state court of appeals may hear cases in which lower court verdicts are challenged. The state also has two federal courts. The U.S. District Court of South Carolina and the U.S. Bankruptcy Court of South Carolina are branches of the national court system. They deal with cases involving federal, not state, laws.

Nationally, South Carolina sends two senators and six congressional representatives to Washington, D.C. Senator J. Strom Thurmond served in the U.S. Senate for forty-six years, longer than anyone else in history. He died at age one hundred in 2003, a few months after retiring from the Senate.

Chapter 4

THE ECONOMY OF SOUTH CAROLINA

About three-fourths of South Carolina workers are in the service sector. It includes government agencies, education, health care, retail businesses, transportation, lodging and dining operations, professional services (lawyers, accountants), banking, and recreational services.

This contrasts starkly with earlier times. During the period of slavery, South Carolina's economy was based largely on plantation crops. Small farms, factories, and businesses also thrived throughout the state during those years.

After the Civil War, the plantation economy was gone—but cotton remained a valuable crop. During the late 1800s, industrialists began building cotton mills across the South. More than 150 operated in South Carolina by 1910. Cotton and other textiles were central to the state's economy throughout the twentieth century.

A job in a cotton mill called for long hours at a very low wage. For many poor families, there was no alternative. Even children worked in mills. "Shoeless Joe" Jackson, the famous baseball player, couldn't go to school because he had to help support his family. In 1894, at age six, he got a job sweeping dust off of mill room floors. Cotton workers in the fields, meanwhile, bent over the rows from dawn until dusk.

Workers in Johns Island sort fresh tomatoes, which will be boxed and distributed to retailers in different parts of the country.

It provided a hard way to earn a living, but cotton was worth more than all other South Carolina field crops combined in the early twentieth century. In 1922, hordes of boll weevils ravaged cotton fields. During the Great Depression of the 1930s, cotton prices fell sharply. Farmers began planting other crops: tobacco, soybeans, grain, and fruit.

Today, peaches, tobacco, peanuts, tomatoes, soybeans, and poultry are leading agricultural products. Cotton continues to be grown throughout the state.

The state's most valuable agricultural asset now, though, is its trees. This is not surprising, considering its great woodlands. Timber has been an important industry since South Carolina's founding.

Recent Economic Changes

The U.S. textile industry declined in the late 1900s. Synthetic materials were replacing cotton cloth, and imported clothing was cheaper than American-made goods. Many U.S. companies moved their textile production overseas. Textile and fiber factories still operate in

South Carolina, but manufacturing in South Carolina today is much more extensive.

During the 1950s, the state government vigorously began recruiting industries from other regions and countries. This economic development has resulted in a wide range of manufacturing. Newer plants produce chemicals, machinery, and many other products.

Industries with major operations or headquarters in South Carolina include automotive (BMW, Michelin), chemical (DuPont, Fujifilm, Celanese, Eastman Chemical), packaging (Sonoco, Cryovac), product distribution (Dollar General, Target), and industrial research (Milliken). In 2009, the Boeing Company announced it would build some of its 787 Dreamliner aircraft in North Charleston. Monster Worldwide opened a massive customer service facility in Florence County for its online job search service.

Government leaders in the mid-twentieth century realized that new industries were creating thousands of job opportunities. The legislature established a statewide technical college system to train workers in various skills. The network now includes sixteen colleges. Students pursue careers not only in factory professions but in health care, computer technology, environmental protection, forest management, business, and many other areas. Almost half the state's higher education students are enrolled at technical colleges.

Approximately forty four-year colleges and universities are likewise important to the economy. They educate students in practically every career field. The oldest institution, the College of Charleston, was established before the American Revolution.

Effective transportation is another plus. Since the 1960s, the Interstate Highway System has been important to practically all of South Carolina's economy. Four interstate highways speed people

PAST
AND
PRESENT

Mixed Ingredients in a Changing Economy

South Carolina enjoys a wide range of economic resources. Agriculture, industry, and tourism are prominent, but none of them alone determines the state's prosperity. There are many other income generators.

For example, South Carolina is a mining state. It is a leading producer of kaolin, a white clay used to make paint, paper, tires, and other goods. Other notable minerals are vermiculite, granite, and limestone. Gold has been mined in many South Carolina locations since the early 1800s.

The fishing industry has faced problems in South Carolina, as it has in other coastal states. Certain fish populations have dwindled, and the waters have become crowded. Still, workboats regularly bring in catches of shellfish (shrimp, clams, etc.) as well as finfish.

Today, as throughout its history, South Carolina is the home of military bases. Their presence has contributed to local economies. Numerous training camps in wartime have brought recruits from around the United States. Since World War I (1914–1918), Fort Jackson (originally Camp Jackson) in Columbia has trained millions of U.S. soldiers. Parris Island in Beaufort County is the oldest U.S. Marine training post. Air force bases operate near Sumter, Charleston, and North.

As in many states, tourism has become big business in South Carolina. It is not a new industry. Since colonial times, visitors have been drawn here from other regions of the country and abroad. Their reports have brought new travelers year by year, in increasing numbers. In the late twentieth century, though, state leaders began focusing especially on tourism. They recognize that South Carolina has many natural, historic, and cultural attractions that appeal to a global audience. Tourists spend billions of dollars in South Carolina every year. This is good for the state's overall economy.

and trucked products in every direction through the state. Major airports are located in Columbia, Greenville-Spartanburg, Charleston, and Myrtle Beach. Charleston is the state's main shipping port.

The annual Spoleto Festival in Charleston is a world-class event. Here, Chinese acrobats entertain crowds in front of Charleston City Hall.

Tourism

The state department of parks, recreation, and tourism estimates twenty-nine million visitors each year. The economic value of tourism to the state is $17 billion annually.

Why do so many people visit South Carolina? Attractions all along the coast account for much of the tourism. From Little River near the North Carolina state line to Hilton Head Island at the southern tip of the state, fresh seafood and recreation (especially golf) bring millions of annual guests. Little River, Georgetown, and other ports offer charter fishing. The Grand Strand along the upper coast, anchored by Myrtle Beach, is famous for its beautiful beaches, splendid variety of world-class entertainment, and—again—golf courses and seafood restaurants.

Scores of historical sites and cultural attractions also bring visitors to the coast. Charleston is one of the South's leading historic cities. Besides its museums, classic architecture, and lovely old plantation gardens, Charleston presents a continuing schedule of cultural events. It is especially known for its spring Spoleto Festival, which showcases performing artists from across the country and abroad. Another historic destination, Georgetown, is South Carolina's third-oldest city.

Beautiful and challenging golf courses are a major tourist attraction. Golfers here take to the eighteenth green at a tournament on Hilton Head Island.

The coast preserves a special part of American history: Gullah culture. Slaves from West Africa during the 1700s blended English with their native languages. They also continued cultural traditions, such as weaving baskets with sweetgrass. Their knowledge of rice cultivation was important to the success of colonial rice plantations.

Farther south, Beaufort, like Georgetown, is a small seaport remarkable for its large, historic homes. Hilton Head has become a prominent resort. It is visited by U.S. presidents and international celebrities—and by ordinary vacationers. Major golf and tennis tournaments are staged at Hilton Head.

Inland, the attractions multiply. Annual equestrian events are popular in Camden, Aiken, and Elloree. Darlington is the scene of NASCAR races and is home of the Stock Car Hall of Fame–Joe Weatherly Museum. The state has forty-two state parks, plus important national parks and historic military sites. More than a hundred festivals and fairs around the state make for a yearlong recreational calendar. Locals and visitors enjoy boating, fishing, skiing, and other water sports, as well as hunting, hiking, camping, and wildlife watching.

Beautiful and challenging golf courses are found throughout South Carolina. The nation's first golf course was established in Charleston in 1786. In Myrtle Beach alone, the number of courses boomed from two in 1950 to more than eighty by the end of the century.

Most towns have at least one museum. The Charleston Museum was the first in the United States, founded in 1773. In Columbia, the South Carolina State Museum is housed in a huge brick building that once was a textile mill. Next to it is the modern EdVenture Children's Museum. Some museums are devoted to history, some to art, some to science, and others to curious themes. They range from farming to African American culture, horseracing, auto racing, boxing, trains, tennis, criminal justice, and dentistry. A museum in Greenville is dedicated to baseball legend "Shoeless Joe" Jackson; it is housed in the cottage where Jackson and his wife lived.

An entertaining Columbia outing might include a visit to the EdVenture Children's Museum and, next door, the South Carolina State Museum.

Greenville, Charleston, Columbia, and Myrtle Beach are noted for their art facilities. Major zoos include Riverbanks Zoo near Columbia and the Greenville Zoo.

Every visitor to South Carolina finds much to occupy a vacation or only a few hours of leisure.

Chapter 5

PEOPLE FROM SOUTH CAROLINA: PAST AND PRESENT

South Carolinians are as diverse as the citizens of any state. Descendants of Native Americans who lived here many centuries ago are here now. Descendants of poor farmers who just wanted to earn a living on small plots of wilderness land are here, too. They are joined by citizens whose ancestors were wealthy planters. Their neighbors include descendants of slaves who worked plantations. Some residents had great-great-great-grandparents who owned stores and shops in cities and villages, who fought in America's wars, who served as teachers and doctors, and who held public offices.

Today, the state receives new residents from other states and foreign countries daily. They come following jobs and the nice year-round climate. Thousands of people retire here every year. Each new arriver enlivens the colorful array of South Carolina's people.

Meet a tiny sample of those, past and present, who have called South Carolina home.

Ben S. Bernanke (1953–) He was appointed U.S. Federal Reserve chairman in 2006. Bernanke was raised in Dillon.

Mary McLeod Bethune (1875–1955) An educator, civil rights activist, and presidential adviser, she was one of

Mary McLeod Bethune, born to a poor farm family, became an adviser to President Franklin D. Roosevelt in the 1940s. After her retirement, Bethune kept writing and speaking about civil rights issues.

seventeen children born near Mayesville to a former slave family. She cofounded Bethune-Cookman College in Florida.

James Brown (1933–2006) The "godfather of soul" was born in Barnwell County.

James F. Byrnes (1879–1972) Born and raised in Charleston, James Byrnes was a U.S. congressman, senator, and Supreme Court justice. He became one of President Franklin D. Roosevelt's closest wartime advisers and top-ranking administration officials.

John C. Calhoun was U.S. vice president during the 1820s. He was a champion of states' rights in the political tension that eventually led to the Civil War.

John C. Calhoun (1782–1850) Calhoun was born in Abbeville District (now Mount Carmel in McCormick County) and became secretary of war under President James Monroe. He was elected vice president of the United States in 1824 and 1828.

Chubby Checker (1941–) Son of a Low Country tobacco farmer, he won instant stardom with his 1960 hit single "The Twist," which started a dance craze.

Valiant South Carolina Women

South Carolina's history books are filled with heroines. Women have accepted challenges and triumphed at critical points in time.

Emily Geiger was a frontier teenager during the Revolutionary War. At a tense point in 1781, she rode almost 100 miles (161 km) on horseback through British-held territory to deliver a message between Patriot commanders. The British caught her—but she memorized the message and ate it before it was discovered. Her captors let her go, and she completed her mission.

Rebecca Motte was a widow who owned a plantation in what is now Calhoun County. British soldiers seized her home, situated on a major supply route, and forced her family to move out. When American forces arrived, they knew they could force the British to surrender only by burning the house. Without hesitation, Motte gave them permission. She even provided flaming arrows for setting the roof ablaze.

During the mid-1800s, the issue of slavery divided the nation. It also divided the South. Sisters Sarah and Angelina Grimké, members of a wealthy Charleston family, moved to Philadelphia and joined the American Antislavery Society. They produced passionate letters and speeches against slavery.

Today, South Carolina women continue to champion difficult causes, publicly and behind the scenes. One of countless examples is Jean Toal of Columbia, who in 1968 became one of the few women lawyers in the state. Some of her court victories helped break gender barriers. She became the first female justice on the state supreme court in 1988. In 2000, she became chief justice.

Mary Boykin Chesnut (1823–1886) She is considered a leading writer of the Confederacy for the detailed, candid diary she kept during the Civil War. She was born on a Stateburg plantation.

Alexander English (1954–) The Columbia native was an NBA scoring leader, eight-time All-Star, and member of the Naismith Basketball Hall of Fame.

Ernest A. Finney Jr. (1931–) In 1985, Ernest Finney became the first African American justice of the state's supreme court in a century. In 1994, Finney became the first African American ever to serve as chief justice.

Joe Frazier (1944–) Known as "Smokin' Joe," the heavy-weight boxing champion is most famous for defeating Muhammad Ali in the 1971 "Fight of the Century." He was born in Beaufort.

Althea Gibson (1927–2003) Althea Gibson, born to a Clarendon County family of sharecroppers, was the first African American to win a tennis title at Wimbledon.

Wil Lou Gray (1883–1984) The Laurens native was a leader in organizing educational programs and schools, especially for illiterate adults and the underprivileged.

Joseph Jefferson Wofford "Shoeless Joe" Jackson (1888–1951) He was born in Pickens County, where his talent in mill league baseball earned him a professional career. Though banned from professional play after the 1919 World Series scandal, he is regarded as one of the greatest players of all time.

Lane Kirkland (1922–1999)
Born in Camden, Lane Kirkland was president of the AFL-CIO labor union from 1979 to 1995.

Eartha Kitt (1927–2008)
The St. Matthews native was a world-renowned stage and screen actress and author. Among other roles, she portrayed Catwoman in the 1960s *Batman* TV series.

Althea Gibson was born in the city of Silver. Gibson was the first African American to be voted the Associated Press's Female Athlete of the Year.

Robert Mills (1781–1855) A Charlestonian, he became a leading architect of his day. Among many other works, his designs include the Washington Monument.

Darla Moore (1953–) Born in Lake City, she is one of the nation's leading businesswomen. The business school at the University of South Carolina is named in her honor.

Julia Peterkin (1880–1961) In 1929, the Laurens County native became the first southern writer to win a Pulitzer Prize for fiction.

Archibald Rutledge (1883–1973) A native of McClellanville, he was South Carolina's first poet laureate. His notable books were *Home by the River* and *God's Children*.

A tragic hero, astronaut Ronald McNair died in the 1986 *Challenger* space shuttle explosion. McNair is shown playing his saxophone while floating in a weightless compartment.

Charles H. Townes (1915–) Born in Greenville, he won the 1964 Nobel Prize in physics for his work on maser and laser development.

A number of South Carolinians have been leaders in America's space program. They include Ronald E. McNair (1950–1986) of Lake City, who died in the 1986 *Challenger* disaster. Charles Duke (1935–) of Lancaster is one of only twelve humans ever to walk on the Moon. Charles Frank Bolden (1946–) of Columbia is a former astronaut who in 2009 became the first permanent African American administrator of NASA.

Timeline

c. 13,000 BCE Humans are believed to have inhabited this region of North America.

c. 100 Early Mississippian Mound Builders live in what is now South Carolina.

1521 The Spaniards are the first Europeans to arrive at the Carolina coast.

1670 The English make the first permanent settlement at Port Royal.

1729 The Carolina territory becomes southern and northern colonies.

1788 South Carolina ratifies the U.S. Constitution and becomes the nation's eighth state.

1790 Columbia replaces Charleston as the state capital.

1828, 1832 Andrew Jackson is elected and reelected president of the United States. Both President Jackson and Vice President John C. Calhoun are native South Carolinians.

1860 South Carolina is the first Southern state to secede from the Union; the Civil War begins shortly afterward.

1876 The election of Wade Hampton as governor ends the Reconstruction era.

1922 A boll weevil invasion destroys much of the state's cotton crop.

1955 Tobacco outstrips cotton as South Carolina's most valuable cash crop.

1960 Blacks in Greenville lead the first antisegregation march in South Carolina.

1989 Hurricane Hugo strikes Charleston and causes great damage several hundred miles inland.

2000 Underwater archaeologists recover the wreck of the Civil War submarine *H. L. Hunley* in Charleston Harbor.

2009 *Library Journal* names the Union County Carnegie Library the Best Small Library in America; the Boeing Company chooses South Carolina as a site for producing its new super-airliner.

2010 In March, performing teachers and students from the world-famous Juilliard School present their second series of concerts and workshops in Aiken, making "Juilliard in Aiken" a unique annual program.

South Carolina at a Glance

State motto:	*Dum Spiro Spero* ("While I Breathe, I Hope")
State capital:	Columbia
State flag:	In 1775, Colonel William Moultrie designed a banner for South Carolina's troops to carry during the Revolution: a silver crescent (new moon) on a blue field. The palmetto tree was added later and represents the state tree. The flag was adopted on January 28, 1861.
State tree:	Palmetto
State bird:	Carolina wren
State flower:	Yellow jessamine
State fruit:	Peach
Statehood date and number:	May 23, 1788; the eighth U.S. state
State nickname:	Palmetto State
Total area and U.S. rank:	31,113 square miles (80,583 sq km); fortieth-largest state
Population:	4,012,000
Length of coastline:	187 miles (301 km) of general coastline; 2,876 miles (4,627 km) of tidal shoreline (including sea islands, tidal inlets, bays, sounds, and river and creek mouths)

State flag

State seal

Highest elevation:	3,560 feet (1,085 m), Sassafras Mountain
Lowest elevation:	0 feet (0 m), Atlantic coast
Major rivers:	Black River, Broad River, Congaree River, Edisto River, Pee Dee River, Saluda River, Savannah River, Wateree River
Major lakes:	Lake Marion, Lake Moultrie, Lake Murray, Lake Wateree, Hartwell Lake, J. Strom Thurmond Lake
Hottest recorded temperature:	111 degrees Farenheit (43.5 degrees Celsius), June 28, 1954, at Camden
Coldest recorded temperature:	-19°F (-28°C), January 21, 1985, at Caesar's Head
Origin of state name:	Named for King Charles I of England
Chief agricultural products:	Tobacco, cotton, soybeans, peaches
Major industries:	Chemicals, industrial equipment, textiles and synthetics, autos and auto-related

Carolina wren

Yellow jessamine

GLOSSARY

adjutant general An army or military unit's chief administrative officer.

blight Widespread plant disease.

ceremonial Created to honor religious or cultural traditions.

circuit court A court that holds sessions in different locations within the same jurisdiction.

comptroller general An official who audits state government finances.

consecutive Events occurring one after another, without interruption.

cultivate To prepare soil and tend crops.

erosion Gradual deterioration of land by wind or water action.

fiber Thread.

Gullah A language and culture found among sea islanders, based on native African traditions.

industrialist The owner or manager of an industry.

magistrate's court A municipal or area court that hears minor cases.

municipality A city or town.

Patriot A supporter of independence during the American Revolution.

persecution Mistreatment of a weaker group of people by those in authority.

plantation A large farm with many resident workers.

populist A politician who appeals to the common people.

probate court A type of court that handles wills and related matters after a person dies.

Reconstruction The period just after the Civil War when the U.S. Army enforced government and order in the South.

secession Withdrawal from an organization or union.

subtropical Located near Earth's warm tropics.

sulfur A useful but foul-smelling chemical.

terrain Land.

textiles Cloths, yarns, and fibers.

Tory A supporter of the British during the American Revolution.

vermiculite A type of mineral that is often used for making insulation.

zoning Local government rules that determine how specific plots of land may be used.

FOR MORE INFORMATION

Clemson University Libraries

Special Collections Unit

Box 343001

Clemson, SC 29634-3001

(864) 656-3031

Web site: http://www.lib.clemson.edu/spcol/schp.html

Collections and displays of the libraries preserve statewide historic and cultural records.

Office of the Governor

P.O. Box 12267

Columbia, SC 29211

(803) 734-2100

Web site: http://www.scgovernor.com

This department offers news and information from the governor's office concerning the economy, education, quality of life, and other statewide concerns.

South Carolina Chamber of Commerce

1201 Main Street, Suite 1700

Columbia, SC 29201

(803) 799-4601

Web site: http://www.scchamber.net

This source provides South Carolina business information.

South Carolina Department of Archives and History

8301 Parklane Road

Columbia, SC 29223

(803) 896-6100

Web site: http://scdah.sc.gov

This department is a key source for historical information about South Carolina.

South Carolina Department of Parks, Recreation, and Tourism

1205 Pendleton Street

Columbia, SC 29201

(803) 734-1700, (866) 224-9339

Web site: http://scprt.com

This is a gateway for visitors to resources for general information and vacation attractions.

South Carolina Historical Society

The Fireproof Building

100 Meeting Street

Charleston, SC 29401

(843) 723-3225

Web site: http://www.southcarolinahistoricalsociety.org

The society is a primary source of state historical material and was founded in 1855.

South Carolina Secretary of State

Edgar Brown Building

205 Edgar Brown Building, Suite 525

Columbia, SC 29201

(803) 734-0629

Web site: http://www.scsos.com

This office provides information about consumer services in South Carolina.

University South Caroliniana Society

910 Sumter Street

Columbia, SC 29208

(803) 777-3131

Web site: http://www.sc.edu/library/socar

The historical library features special collections housed at the University of South Carolina.

Web Sites

Due to the changing nature of Internet links, Rosen Publishing has developed an online list of Web sites related to the subject of this book. This site is updated regularly. Please use this link to access the list:

http://www.rosenlinks.com/uspp/scpp

Bass, Jack, and W. Scott Poole. *The Palmetto State: The Making of Modern South Carolina*. Columbia, SC: University of South Carolina Press, 2009.

Edgar, Walter. *South Carolina: A History*. Columbia, SC: University of South Carolina Press, 1998.

Hasan, Heather. *A Primary Source History of the Colony of South Carolina* (Primary Sources of the Thirteen Colonies and the Lost Colony). New York, NY: Rosen Publishing Group, 2006.

Megginson, W. J. *African American Life in South Carolina's Upper Piedmont, 1780–1900*. Columbia, SC: University of South Carolina Press, 2006.

Somervill, Barbara A. *South Carolina* (America the Beautiful). New York, NY: Scholastic, 2009.

South Carolina: The Palmetto State (Discover America). Chicago, IL: Encyclopedia Britannica, Inc., 2005.

Stroud, Cynthia Mitchell. *Carolina Children: The Sandhills*. Mauldin, SC: Carolina Children's Press, 2007.

Weatherly, Myra S. *South Carolina* (From Sea to Shining Sea). New York, NY: Children's Press, 2009.

Weiner, Roberta, and James R. Arnold. *South Carolina: The History of South Carolina Colony, 1670–1776* (13 Colonies). Chicago, IL: Raintree, a Division of Reed Elsevier, Inc., 2005.

Worth, Richard. *South Carolina* (Life in the Thirteen Colonies). New York, NY: Children's Press, 2004.

BIBLIOGRAPHY

Bache, Ben. *South Carolina: Great Stories That Embrace the History of the Palmetto State.* Greenville, SC: Homecourt Publishers, 2005.

Beck, Evelyn. "Tuning in to Technical Education: South Carolina's Technical College System Offers Smart Career Options & Avocational Pursuits for Students of All Ages." *Sandlapper Magazine*, Autumn 2008, pp. 43–44.

Edgar, Walter, ed. *The South Carolina Encyclopedia.* Columbia, SC: The Humanities Council[SC]/University of South Carolina Press, 2006.

Environmental Defense Fund. "South Carolina's Coast: What's at Stake." May 29, 2007. Retrieved October 5, 2009 (http://www.edf.org/article.cfm?contentid=5377).

Flowers, Julie. "Tourism Development in SC." Columbia, SC: South Carolina Department of Parks, Recreation and Tourism presentation, June 2009.

Harmon, Daniel E. "RedCliffe: The Double Life of a Plantation Population." *Sandlapper Magazine*, Winter 2009–2010, pp. 52–54.

Harmon, Daniel E. "REVOLUTION: South Carolina at War." *Sandlapper Magazine*, Autumn 2004 through Winter 2005–2006.

Harmon, Daniel E. "A Visit with the Legendary 'Shoeless Joe.'" *Boiling Springs Today*, April 2009, pp. 18–19.

Lander, Ernest McPherson Jr., and Archie Vernon Huff Jr. *South Carolina: An Illustrated History of the Palmetto State.* Sun Valley, CA: American Historical Press, 2007.

McLaughlin, J. Michael, and Lee Davis Jodman. *It Happened in South Carolina.* Guilford, CT: TwoDot, 2004.

Pew Environment Group. "Miles of South Carolina Coastline at Stake." Save the Lowcountry, February 10, 2009. Retrieved October 5, 2009 (http://www.pewglobal warming.org/savethelowcountry/pr_10-feb-2009.html).

South Carolina Department of Parks, Recreation, and Tourism. "Fast Facts About South Carolina." Retrieved October 4, 2009 (http://www.scprt.com/facts-figures/helpwith homework/fastfacts.aspx).

Townsend, Kenneth. *South Carolina* (On-the-Road Histories). Northampton, MA: Interlink Books, 2009.

U.S. Geological Survey. "South Carolina: Earthquake History." Retrieved November 2009 (http://earthquake.usgs.gov/earthquakes/states/south_carolina/history.php).

INDEX

A

Ali, Muhammad, 36
American Revolution, 5, 16, 17–18, 27, 35

B

Bernanke, Ben S., 32
Bethune, Mary McLeod, 32
boll weevil invasion, 26
Brown, James, 34
Byrnes, James F., 34

C

Calhoun, John C., 34
Checker, Chubby, 34
Chestnut, Mary Boykin, 36
civil rights, 5, 20, 23, 32
Civil War, 5, 16, 19, 23, 25, 36
Congaree National Park, 11

E

Edwards, James B., 20
English, Alexander, 36

F

Finney Jr., Ernest A., 36
Frazier, Joe, 36

G

Gibson, Althea, 36
Gray, Wil Lou, 36
Great Depression, 26
Gullah culture, 30

H

Hampton, Wade, 18–19
Hilton Head Island, 29, 30
H. L. Hunley, 16
Hurricane Hugo, 11

J

Jackson, Jesse, 20
Jackson, "Shoeless Joe," 25, 31, 36–37

K

Kirkland, Lane, 37
Kitt, Eartha, 37
Ku Klux Klan, 18

L

Lincoln, Abraham, 18

M

McNair, Ronald E., 38
Mills, Robert, 37
Monroe, James, 34
Moore, Darla, 37
Myrtle Beach, 29, 30, 31

N

Native Americans, 5, 8, 13, 14, 15, 32

P

Peterkin, Julia, 38
Poinsett, Joel R., 10, 16

About the Author

Daniel E. Harmon is the author of more than seventy books and thousands of magazine and newspaper articles. He has written two other books in this series, *Washington: Past and Present* and *Minnesota: Past and Present*. His geographical and historical books also include a profile of the Hudson River, works on the exploration of America and other parts of the world, and studies of numerous world nations. Harmon has been an editor for *Sandlapper: The Magazine of South Carolina* since 1981. He lives in Spartanburg, South Carolina.

Photo Credits

Cover (top left) SSPL via Getty Images; cover (top right) Ralph Mayer, Lexington, SC; cover (bottom), p. 9 Altrendo/Getty Images; pp. 3, 6, 13, 21, 25, 32, 39 © www.istock photo.com/catnap72; p. 4 (top) © GeoAtlas; pp. 7, 41 (left) Shutterstock.com; p. 8 Doug Collier/AFP/Getty Images; p. 12 Alan Weiner/Getty Images; pp. 14, 37 Hulton Archive/ Getty Images; p. 18 Stock Montage/Hulton Archive/Getty Images; p. 19 Steve Liss/Time & Life Pictures/Getty Images; p. 22 Wikimedia Commons (http://en.wikipedia.org/wiki/ South_Carolina_State_House); p. 26 Stephen Morton/Getty Images; p. 29 © AP Images; p. 30 Streeter Lecka/Getty Images; p. 31 © 2009 Photo by Kerry Johnston/EdVenture Children's Museum; p. 33 Gordon Parks/Hulton Archive/Getty Images; p. 34 MPI/ Hulton Archive/Getty Images; p. 38 NASA/Hulton Archive/Getty Images; p. 40 (left) Courtesy of Robesus, Inc.; p. 41 (right) Jeff McMillian © USDA-NRCS PLANTS Database.

Designer: Les Kanturek; Editor: Kathy Kuhtz Campbell;
Photo Researcher: Karen Huang